Explore Duluth OUTDOORS

HIKING

BIKING

& MORE

MENASHA RIDGE PRESS
Your Guide to the Outdoors Since 1982

Paul Kautz

T0166288

About the Author

Paul Kautz writes books and blogs when he's not out hiking. He also presents Wilderness First Aid, Leave No Trace, and lightweight backpacking training to people preparing for their adventures. Paul is the owner of Active Source, Inc. and lives in Eden Prairie, Minnesota, with his wife.

DEDICATION

In memory of Aaron. Yours was a trail too short.
We love and miss you.

Explore Duluth Outdoors: Your Guide to Hiking, Biking, and More

Copyright © 2018 by Paul Kautz
All rights reserved
Published by Menasha Ridge Press
Distributed by Publishers Group West
Printed in China
First edition, first printing

ISBN 978-1-63404-110-2; eISBN 978-1-63404-111-9

Design: Lora Westberg
Photos: Contributed by Aaron de Venecia and the author
Copy editors: Tim Jackson and Holly Cross
Proofreader: Emily Beaumont
Typesetting: Monica Ahlman
Cartography: Scott McGrew

Menasha Ridge Press
An imprint of AdventureKEEN
2204 First Ave. S., Ste. 102
Birmingham, Alabama 35233

Visit menasharidge.com for a complete listing of our books and for ordering information. Contact us at our website, at facebook.com/menasharidge, or at twitter.com/menasharidge with questions or comments. To find out more about who we are and what we're doing, visit our blog, blog.menasharidge.com.

Front cover: Lester River by www.jonwoodphoto.com

Introduction

Duluth offers an endless array of outdoor activities that make it one of Minnesota's most popular destinations. From the shore of Lake Superior, Duluth climbs 800 feet up a rocky hillside and spreads into the great north woods. This unique location provides wonderful terrain for rock climbing, mountain biking, alpine and cross-country skiing, and hiking.

The Duluth harbor attracts millions of visitors each year, many coming to watch the hundreds of freight ships that use the port, some of which come all the way from the Atlantic Ocean 2,342 miles away. Other visitors tour the aquarium or zoo, drive the Skyline Parkway across Duluth with views of the lake, or take a scenic train ride along the north shore.

With more than 100 public parks, gardens, and forests featuring hundreds of miles of bike trails, snowmobile trails, ski trails, and hiking trails, there is room for everyone to enjoy the city. The layout of Duluth creates three styles of trail: flat and busy down by the lake, secluded rolling hills up in the woods, and rugged and steep between the two. Dozens of creeks drain the high land through gorges cut into the bedrock and create rushing rapids and cascading waterfalls to explore, hidden from the commotion of the surrounding city.

For refueling, relaxing, and resting after a busy day outdoors, Duluth has many restaurants and hotels, a handful of craft breweries, and even a craft distillery.

While many of the locations featured in this book are suitable for multiple outdoors activities, if the area is especially known for specific pursuits, we've listed them on the page using the indicators to the right.

HIKING
BIKING
SKIING
CLIMBING
SWIMMING

Lakewalk

BREWER PARK

HIKING
BIKING
CLIMBING

Get an early start to hike this popular lollipop loop on the hills overlooking the city.

Difficulty: Moderate

Length/Time: 3.5 miles; 2–3 hours

Hours/Fees: Open 24/7; free

Getting There: *2588 Haines Rd.* Take Exit 253B off I-35. Head northwest on S 40th Ave. for 1.7 miles as it turns into Haines Rd. After passing Skyline Pkwy., look for a paved parking area on the right. GPS: N46.7624°, W92.1701°

Contact: 218-730-4300, duluthmn.gov/parks/parks-listing/brewer-park-bellevue-park

Additional Information: Walk up the sidewalk and cross under Haines Road through an underground walkway. Refer to trail signage after exiting the underpass to ensure you use the hiking trail rather than the biking trail, which is also used by many mountain bikers moving between Brewer and Piedmont trail systems.

When the trail levels somewhat, it will split. Take the path on the right to save the best views for later. When you intersect with the main Superior Hiking Trail, turn left and follow the trail back toward your starting point. You can look down the steep hillside to the St. Louis River and Duluth-Superior harbor. Because this well-signed trail is on a high hilltop, there are no water sources or facilities. Be sure to bring your own water and snacks.

The park also includes 5 miles of mountain bike trail and a few rock-climbing spots.

This rugged trail follows a rough and tumbling creek with many rapids and waterfalls.

Difficulty: Strenuous

Length/Time: 4 miles; 2–3 hours

Hours/Fees: Open 24/7; free

Getting There: *1329 E. 4th St.* Take Exit 258 off I-35. Turn left on S. 21st Ave E. and travel 0.6 mile. Turn left on E. 4th St. and drive 0.6 mile. Park on the street at the intersection with S. 14th Ave. E. GPS: N46.8030º, W92.0850º

Contact: 218-730-4300, duluthmn.gov/parks/parks-listing/chester-park

Additional Information: Enter the park on a path between rock barricades, following the northwest bank of Chester Creek. The trail soon becomes rougher dirt and rock, and it can be wet and slippery.

As you climb along the creek, you are walking on rock over 1 billion years old. The rapids and small waterfalls along the way have been slowly carving this rock since the great glacial Lake Duluth receded 10,000 years ago.

Walk under the 9th Street bridge. When you reach Skyline Parkway, you enter the Chester Bowl area. Here, you can take a break at the picnic area or play on the playground equipment.

From the picnic area, walk uphill on the road until it ends at an activity field. Follow the left edge of the field to the far side to the trail heading up into the forest. Follow the trail along the creek and cross on a footbridge, then stay to the right. The trail eventually opens out onto the ski hill. Follow the path down to reach the creek near the bottom of the ski hill. Stay with the trail on the near bank of the creek to return to your starting point.

Chester Bowl offers a challenging cross-country ski route and inexpensive downhill course in the winter.

CONGDON PARK

Waterfalls, rapids, bridges, and trees are all here for you to explore.
This park is great for kids!

Difficulty: Moderate

Length/Time: 1.5 miles; 1 hour

Hours/Fees: Open 24/7; free

Getting There: *3290 E. 1st St.* From MN 61 heading north, turn left onto S. 32nd Ave. E. At the T intersection, turn right onto Congdon Park Dr. and travel 0.3 mile, crossing E. Superior St. Park by the intersection with E. 1st St. GPS: N46.8185°, W92.0585°

Contact: 218-730-4300, duluthmn.gov/parks/parks-listing/congdon-park

Additional Information: To explore the most interesting bits, head downhill on the trail starting at the corner of Congdon Park Drive and East 1st Street. After exploring, take any branch in the trail to your left from the creek to run into Congdon Park Drive and take it back to your car.

For a longer hike, head uphill on the gravel trail by the creek for 0.25 mile to cross East 4th Street. Continue 0.35 mile to the top of the park at Vermilion Road. Turn right, and then immediately turn right again onto Lakeview Drive. Find the trail entrance on your right.

Follow this rugged trail downstream to East 4th Street. Turn right on the road to cross the creek and then left onto the trail to return to the start.

There are no facilities around but plenty of water to filter from the creek. There are dozens of places to stop and cool your feet in the creek too.

The many small waterfalls continually work away at the hard bedrock, much of which is red rhyolite. The man-made bridges, staircases, and trail make this hike even more interesting.

Pass through an abandoned railroad tunnel and explore old trestles.

Difficulty: Easy

Length/Time: 1–13 miles; 1 hour to all day

Hours/Fees: Open 24/7; free

Getting There: *Becks Road.* Take Exit 246 from I-35 onto Midway Rd. and head south 2.3 miles. On the left, there is a gravel parking area at the trailhead. If you cross railroad tracks on a bridge, you've gone too far. GPS: N46.6802°, W92.2601°

Contact: 218-730-4316, duluthmn.gov/st-louis-river-corridor /dwp-trail-corridor

Additional Information: Follow the boardwalk and stairs for 0.1 mile to the abandoned DWP railbed. Turn right and walk 0.2 mile to the tunnel. The tunnel is 0.1 mile long. From the tunnel, the trail continues 2.7 miles to an abandoned bridge over Stewart Creek. You can turn back here for a 6.2-mile hike or walk across the trestle to continue. Another 1.1 miles brings you to an open break in the woods at the base of Spirit Mountain. Head back for an 8.5-mile hike or follow the trail 2.2 miles to its endpoint on Green Street just after passing under I-35 for a 13-mile-long day of hiking.

The tunnel is definitely the highlight of this route, with the sounds of wind, dripping water, and rocks being clacked together echoing in the darkness. It's short enough that a smartphone flashlight app is adequate, or bring a regular, handheld flashlight. Kids love this short adventure.

Rock climbers love to scale the tunnel entrance. You may notice the permanent bolts in the ceiling.

ELY'S PEAK

Scramble up a short, rocky outcrop to impressive views of Duluth's west side, the St. Louis River, and Wisconsin.

Difficulty: Strenuous

Length/Time: 2 miles; 1–2 hours

Hours/Fees: Open 24/7; free

Getting There: *123rd Ave. W.* Take Exit 246 from I-35 onto Midway Road heading south. Follow Midway, which turns into Becks Road, for 2.7 miles. After crossing the railroad tracks, turn left onto 123rd Ave. W. Follow this gravel road 1,000 feet to a parking area. GPS: N46.6761°, W92.2588°

Contact: None

Additional Information: Walk north on the trail for 0.1 mile. Turn right on the paved Munger Trail and follow it southeast for 0.4 mile, looking for the blue-blazed Superior Hiking Trail branching to the left, heading uphill. There should be a sign here, just about 0.1 mile after crossing the bridge over the railroad tracks. Follow the trail uphill through forest and open rocky areas for 0.4 mile. Near the top, look for a spur trail turning sharply to the left and continuing uphill as the main trail forges ahead and begins to go downhill. Another 0.1 mile on the spur brings you to the wide-open summit. There are many open spots around the top to rest and even have a picnic.

You will most likely find many other people around the summit and on the trail at this popular location, especially in the fall when the forest below becomes a carnival of colors.

Climbers will enjoy the many bouldering opportunities on the rock outcrops on this small mountain.

HIKING
CLIMBING

From the top of Enger Tower, you can see forever.

Difficulty: Moderate

Length/Time: 1 mile; 1–2 hours

Hours/Fees: Closed in winter; free

Getting There: *1461 W. Skyline Pkwy.* Take Exit 255A on I-35 to head northwest on US 53 for 1.1 miles. Turn left onto W. 10th St., then right onto N. 24th Ave. W for 0.25 mile. Turn right onto W. Skyline Pkwy. and travel 1.5 miles to the paved Twin Ponds trailhead parking lot on the right. GPS: N46.7787°, W92.1229°

Contact: 218-730-4300, duluthmn.gov/parks/parks-listing/enger-park

Additional Information: Cross Skyline Parkway and walk around the pond. Cross a tiny footbridge, climb the steps, and cross Skyline Parkway again, following the trail uphill. At a roofed structure, you enter the park. This first shelter houses a very popular Japanese Peace Bell, gifted to Duluth from its sister city of Isumi-Ohara. You know you want to ring it, so go ahead! Really, it's OK, and even expected.

Walk south from here to enjoy the many gardens. At the main park building, walk east on the trail to find a Japanese gazebo. The trail out of the gazebo takes you up to a parking area. Cross this parking area and walk toward the exit, looking for the dirt trail leading up to Enger Tower. Built in 1939, the 80-foot-tall tower rises five stories above the summit, offering 360-degree views. The tower has an internal staircase, allowing visitors to climb to the top. The paved trail leading down from the north side of the tower takes you back to the main park building.

The east side of this hill is a popular bouldering spot, especially for beginners. Hundreds of migrating raptors can be viewed from here in March and April.

HARTLEY PARK

This popular nature preserve was farmland 100 years ago.

Difficulty: Moderate

Length/Time: 3.5 miles; 2–3 hours

Hours/Fees: Trails open 24/7; nature center open 9 a.m.–5 p.m. Monday–Friday and 10 a.m.–5 p.m. Saturday. Free

Getting There: *3001 Woodland Ave.* Take Exit 258 from I-35 onto S. 21st Ave. E., heading northwest uphill for 0.7 mile. Turn right onto Woodland Ave. and follow it 2.4 miles. Turn left onto Hartley Rd. and travel 0.25 mile to the entrance. GPS: N46.8385°, W92.0821°

Contact: 218-724-6735, hartleynature.org

Additional Information: From the nature center, follow Hartley Park Trail west for 0.2 mile and turn left, crossing the dam. Follow the blue-blazed trail east for 0.9 mile, mostly uphill and then along a ridge. Turn left when you drop to the wide, gravel Hartley Road Trail to follow the blue blazes. In about 70 yards, follow the blue-blazed trail as it splits to the right. At the next split in 100 yards, take the trail on the right, leaving the blue-blazed trail. Follow it 0.5 mile along the edge of a forest. Turn right onto the Meadow Trail going northeast for 0.5 mile.

At a trail intersection, as you are hiking uphill, turn right to continue 0.1 mile to the top of Rock Knob. Look for a trail going steeply downhill to the southeast and follow it 0.1 mile until it flattens. Turn left (northeast) onto the Hartley Road Trail and walk 0.5 mile back to the parking lot.

These are multiuse trails shared with bicyclists in summer and cross-country skiers in winter. Because they are so well used, trails are very easy to navigate, but the many intersections can be tricky. The nature center rents skis and snowshoes and has restrooms, water, and vending machines.

View migrating birds of prey after enjoying a secluded forest stream on this hike.

Difficulty: Moderate

Length/Time: 4 miles; 2–3 hours

Hours/Fees: Open any time; Free

Getting There: *E. Skyline Pkwy.* Take Exit 259 off I-35 to merge onto MN 61 northbound for 3.3 miles. Turn left onto N. 60th Ave. E. In three blocks, turn right onto E. Superior St. Take the next left onto Occidental Blvd. and travel uphill for 1.8 winding miles. When the road makes a U-turn at the Maxwell Rd. intersection and crosses one more bridge, park in the gravel trailhead on the right. GPS: N46.8607°, W92.0163°

Contact: 218-428-6209, hawkridge.org

Additional Information: Walk uphill on the obvious Snively Trail as it follows Amity Creek on a multiuse trail shared with mountain bikers. At about 1.3 miles, when power lines cross overhead, find a dirt trail leading steeply uphill to your left. Follow it a couple hundred feet until it splits. Take the right fork, which is the Amity Trail, into the forest. At the trail intersection where there is a boardwalk, turn right onto Ole's Trail to leave the forest and reach the bird observation platform. Follow the trail downhill to Skyline Parkway and turn left for an easy stroll back to the trailhead.

The best bird-watching is mid-August through October, with thousands of hawks, eagles, falcons, and other birds flying overhead. During birding season, there are portable toilets on Skyline Parkway. The only water is in Amity Creek, so bring your own or filter some before climbing the ridge.

Kids will do well on this hike, as it has plenty of exploring potential and no overly strenuous areas. Save the bird-viewing area for the end so they have something to look forward to.

JAY COOKE STATE PARK

History, nature, architecture, and many miles of trail options make this park interesting for everyone. It is a big attraction for visitors throughout the year.

Difficulty: Easy

Length/Time: 4+ miles; 2+ hours

Hours/Fees: Daily, 8 a.m.–10 p.m.; $5 state park fee

Getting There: *780 MN 210, Carlton.* Take I-35 south from Duluth for about 15 miles. Exit 242 from I-35 onto Thomson Rd. heading south. Turn left at the T intersection with MN 210 and follow it 1.75 miles to the Swinging Bridge Area entrance on the right. GPS: N46.6550°, W92.3726°

Contact: 218-673-7000, dnr.state.mn.us/state_parks/jay_cooke

Additional Information: Cross the 220-foot-long swinging suspension bridge over the St. Louis River. ♿ Stay to the left at every trail junction so you are on the River Trail heading downstream. After 1.5 miles, at junction 38, turn right to take the Summer Trail for 0.5 mile south and then 1 mile northwest to trail junction 35. At all marked junctions, follow the signs back to the visitor center, where you'll find water and restrooms.

Alternatively, you can get a map at the visitor center and check out many other parts of the park. Summer and winter trail maps for hiking, biking, skiing, and horseback riding are available. This is a great place to spend an entire day exploring.

The river is the main attraction, and the bridge area can be busy. The backcountry trails mostly traverse the hardwood forest and provide a bit more solitude. In fall the spectacular colors from maple, poplar, and oak trees are interspersed with various pine and fir trees.

Find remnants of old roads lost to an encroaching forest while cascading waters tumble past.

Difficulty: Strenuous

Length/Time: 3 miles; 2 hours

Hours/Fees: Open 24/7; free

Getting There: *7214 Waseca St.* Take Exit 251B from I-35 onto Grand Ave. and head west for 0.9 mile. Turn right onto Waseca St. and drive 0.2 mile to the end. GPS: N46.7274°, W92.1906°

Contact: www.duluthgov.info/parks/trail_pages/kingsbury_creek_trail.cfm

Additional Information: Follow the path west along the zoo fence under pine trees to its intersection with the DWP Trail. Take the path up the creek, crossing the bridge at 0.25 mile, and then continue uphill along the creek for 0.7 mile. When the main trail, marked by blue blazes, veers left at 0.7 mile, continue following it across the hillside for 0.85 mile. When it intersects with a dirt road at Knowlton Creek, turn left and follow it downhill along the creek for about 0.5 mile. Stay with the road as it veers away from the creek to the left and becomes improved. When the main road turns right in 0.2 mile, stay straight ahead, walking across the hillside rather than downhill. Reach the first bridge you crossed in 0.5 mile to complete the loop.

This trail is quite steep and rugged along the creek, but the hillside walk is much easier. Kids will have more fun exploring the short creek loop, and everyone will enjoy cooling their feet in the creek at the end or stopping at the zoo for a treat.

Public bathrooms and water are available at the zoo when it is open. A nice picnic area and playground near the trailhead allow for relaxing after your hike.

LAKEWALK

Immerse yourself in the Duluth culture in the center of it all.

Difficulty: Easy

Length/Time: 4.5–6 miles; 2–4 hours

Hours/Fees: Open 24/7; free

Getting There: *2025 E. Water St.* Take Exit 258 off I-35 and turn right onto S. 23rd Ave. E. At the first intersection, turn right onto E. Water St. and follow it to the parking lot on the north side. GPS: N46.8029°, W92.0681°

Contact: 218-730-4300, duluthmn.gov/parks/parks-listing/lakewalk

Additional Information: Walk or bike southwest from the parking lot on the paved trail that runs beside the lake. After 0.8 mile, you'll go under a pedestrian overpass. Cross this bridge to Leif Erickson Park and Rose Gardens.

Cross back over the bridge to continue through the rest of Leif Erikson Park. After another 0.7 mile, you will come to the Duluth Veterans Memorial area. Just past the memorials, cross the railroad tracks and turn left to explore Lake Place Park. Then, take the ramp down toward the shoreline where the Lakewalk continues south, now a boardwalk. Continue 0.3 mile to reach the Aerial Lift Bridge. ♿

Before heading back, you could walk over the lift bridge, visit the free Lake Superior Maritime Center, or walk the 800 feet to the lighthouse at the end of the pier for an interesting view back toward shore.

Return to your starting spot along the same path, hugging the lake shore and using the boardwalk when present rather than the paved surface.

There are public restrooms and water by Sister Cities Park and at the Rose Gardens. For lunch, you might try one of the many restaurants available in the Canal Park area, but be aware that this is a popular idea, especially during summer, so hundreds of other visitors will probably have the same plan.

This is a beautiful park that is secret to no one but has room for everyone, even the occasional moose.

Difficulty: Easy

Length/Time: 1–7 miles; 30 minutes–4 hours

Hours/Fees: Open 24/7; free

Getting There: *Lester River Rd.* Take Exit 259 off I-35 to merge onto MN 61 northbound for 3.3 miles. Turn left onto N. 60th Ave. E. In three blocks, turn right onto E. Superior St. In two blocks, turn left onto Lester River Rd. and park on the left. GPS: N46.8403°, W92.0061°

Contact: 218-730-4300, duluthmn.gov/parks/parks-listing/lester-park

Additional Information: Cross a footbridge over the Lester River and walk west across the park for 50 yards until you reach Amity Creek. Turn right and follow the trail up the creek for about 0.3 mile to a bridge. Head northeast to a junction with a trail map labeled "A."

For more exploring, follow the ski trails for as far as you'd like to hike. For a shorter loop, follow the eastern trail uphill 0.25 mile, where a hiking trail splits to the right off the wide ski trail. Follow this trail about 0.2 mile to a bridge over the river. Turn right and follow the river trail back to your start.

There are many miles of mountain bike trails and cross-country ski trails throughout this park. It is the eastern end of the Duluth Traverse bike trail. This is a great place for having a picnic, swimming, and enjoying the playground with your kids. Also keep in mind that this park is extremely popular and busy.

This nice hike follows the bank of Miller Creek.

Difficulty: Moderate

Length/Time: 2 miles; 1 hour

Hours/Fees: Open 24/7; free

Getting There: *Lincoln Park Dr.* Take Exit 254 off I-35 onto S. 27th Ave. W. heading northwest and uphill for 0.4 mile. Turn right onto W. 3rd St. and drive 1 block. Turn left onto Lincoln Park Dr. to enter the park. GPS: N46.7660°, W92.1351°

Contact: 218-730-4300, duluthmn.gov/parks/parks-listing/lincoln-park

Additional Information: Starting at the playground, walk up Lincoln Park Drive to the first bridge over Miller Creek. Turn off the roadway to the right just before the bridge to continue on the dirt trail up the right side of the creek. When you pop out onto N. 24th Ave W., turn around and head back down the way you hiked up.

When you reach the bridge crossing the creek where the trail started, cross it and follow the paved trail on the northwest corner of the bridge downhill through the manicured park. This takes you past Elephant Rock, which is worth a closer look, and on to the huge stonework pavilion. ♿

As you're walking through the park, you might try to locate all nine holes of the disc golf course. You may also notice the painted tee boxes on the pavement.

Back at your car, it's a great time to have a picnic, spend time on the playground equipment, or wade in the creek.

Enjoy old-growth forest, spectacular views, a monument, and a stone arch bridge at Magney-Snively.

Difficulty: Moderate

Length/Time: 3+ miles; 2+ hours

Hours/Fees: Open 24/7; free

Getting There: *W. Skyline Pkwy.* Take Exit 249 off I-35 onto W. Skyline Pkwy. Head south 0.4 mile to a T intersection. Turn left, staying on Skyline Pkwy. for 2 more miles. Find the Magney-Snively Trailhead parking on the left after crossing Stewart Creek. GPS: N46.7020°, W92.2272°

Contact: 218-730-4300, duluthmn.gov/parks/parks-listing /magney-snivey-natural-area

Additional Information: Cross Skyline Parkway to the trail leading up the hill. For a 3-mile loop to Bardon Peak, follow the trail about 0.5 mile through intersection "A." Turn left at intersection "B." Follow the trail as it crosses the Superior Hiking Trail in 0.5 mile and again in 0.25 mile. In another 0.3 mile, the trail opens onto a rocky outcrop on Bardon Peak. Continue on the trail as it makes a U-turn north for about 1 mile to the "D" T intersection. Veer right (northeast) to follow the path back to the trailhead, or explore more of the forest.

From the parking area, walk east along Skyline Parkway for 0.15 mile over the stone arch bridge to visit the Snively Memorial.

Your hike will take you through a wild forest of oak, maple, birch, basswood, ironwood, and other trees. The diverse forest provides great habitat for wildlife, which you'll most likely hear, if not actually see.

This natural area is enjoyed by hikers, equestrians, cross-country skiers, and snowmobilers, but there are no mountain bike trails.

MILLENNIUM TRAIL

HIKING
BIKING

Bike or stroll through a fragrant boreal forest with rest stops and interpretive signs.

Difficulty: Easy

Length/Time: 2.8 miles; 1–2 hours

Hours/Fees: Open 24/7; free

Getting There: *N. 28th St. and Wyoming Ave.* Take Exit 253A from I-35 to merge onto US 2 south and cross the bridge into Wisconsin. Turn right onto Belknap St. at the roundabout. Follow Belknap west for 3 blocks. Turn left onto Wyoming Ave. and follow it 1 mile to its end. Continue straight ahead into the parking area. GPS: N46.705373°, W92.123759°

Contact: ci.superior.wi.us/235/Trails

Additional Information: From the parking lot, follow the paved trail due west to its western terminus at Billings Drive and back. There are plans to extend the trail in the future. ♿

Along the trail, you will find tall prairie grass; pine, cedar, birch, and aspen trees; and various shrubs and brush. This quiet woods is alive with animals and birds.

This walk includes a handful of small interpretive signs spaced along the route so visitors can learn about the flora and fauna. Benches have also been installed so you can sit and listen as long as you'd like.

To explore more, there are miles of ski trails in the Superior Municipal Forest, but they are not maintained in summer. To see some trains, head east from the parking area on the arrow-straight Millennium Trail for 0.4 mile to the terminus at Elmira Avenue. Ahead is a railroad yard with 35 tracks. Walk 100 yards north to N. 28th Street and then east for a closer view of the trains.

HIKING
SWIMMING

Explore the world's longest freshwater sandbar on this flat trail separating Superior Bay from Lake Superior.

Difficulty: Easy

Length/Time: 4 miles; 2 hours

Hours/Fees: Open 24/7; free

Getting There: *5098 Minnesota Ave.* Take Exit 256B from I-35 and turn left onto S. Lake Ave. Take the next right onto W. Railroad St. and then the next left back onto S. Lake Ave. Follow Lake Ave. as it jogs right in 1 mile, changing into Minnesota Ave. Find trailhead parking by Sky Harbor Airport. GPS: N46.7272°, W92.0473°

Contact: 218-730-4300, duluthmn.gov/parks/parks-listing/park-point

Additional Information: The nature trail begins directly left of the first airport building, through a pedestrian opening next to a chain-link gate. Follow the sand-and-gravel trail southeast along the airport fence for 0.4 mile, then veer left into the forest. At about 1.2 miles, the forest opens to grassy sand dunes. Stick to the most worn path to pass the Zero Point lighthouse tower at about 1.6 miles. This is the oldest standing structure in Duluth. Just after the lighthouse, a small forested area hides an abandoned boathouse.

The last quarter mile of trail is open, sandy grassland. Take any path back to your car. Just keep the bay on your left and the lake on your right.

This hike can be done any time of year. The nearby water provides an opportunity to cool off on hot days, and though there are few fall colors, there is much less traffic in the fall.

After your hike, you can use the public restrooms at Park Point, have a picnic, or swim at the beach.

The Osaugie Trail features sweeping views of Superior Bay, large ships, and the trains and structures that load their cargo.

Difficulty: Easy

Length/Time: 1–10 miles; 30 minutes–3 hours

Hours/Fees: Open 24/7; free

Getting There: *305 E. 2nd St., Superior, WI.* Take Exit 255B from I-35 onto US 53 south over the bridge for 2.5 miles to Superior, Wisconsin. Exit immediately to stay on US 53 and travel southeast for 1.7 miles. Turn left at the streetlight to enter the Veteran's Historical Center parking lot. GPS: N46.7230°, W92.0691°

Contact: ci.superior.wi.us/235/Trails

Additional Information: From the trail archway between the historical center and the playground, follow the paved trail south as far as you'd like. You can't get lost. The trailhead area will most likely have other visitors, but the farther you venture, the fewer people you'll meet. This is a nice trail for cyclists. ♿

The trail extends 5 miles southeast paralleling US 2, but from there it becomes the gravel Tri-County Corridor trail, which continues for another 65 miles to Ashland. The first 2.6 miles to the Nemadji River bridge are the most interesting. You can see big cargo ships coming and going in the farthest inland freshwater seaport in North America.

The playground where you started is perfect for a posthike picnic.

HIKING
BIKING
SKIING

This hike offers solitude and quiet on wide ski trails with a surprise view toward the end.

Difficulty: Moderate

Length/Time: 3 miles; 1-2 hours

Hours/Fees: Open 24/7; free

Getting There: *2290 Hutchinson Rd.* Exit 255A from I-35 to head northwest on US 53 for 1.4 miles. Turn left onto Piedmont Ave., and then left again onto Hutchinson Rd. Drive 0.6 mile to the paved parking area on the left. GPS: N46.7744°, W92.1574°

Contact: 218-730-4300, duluthmn.gov/parks/parks-listing/piedmont-park

Additional Information: This is a great get-away-from-it-all walk through the woods. Enter the forest on the obvious trail. Keep in mind that it can be tricky to navigate this area because it has many intersecting trails for hiking, skiing, snowmobiles, and mountain bikes. Hikers should stay off the mountain bike trails. Just remember to stay on the wide doubletrack trail. If a narrow trail crosses your path, ignore it. If another wide doubletrack trail crosses, always take the right-hand path to make a long, winding loop back to the trailhead.

The high point of the trail is Piedmont Knob, with great views of Duluth. About 2 miles out, the woods open up and you can explore onto a rock outcrop before continuing your loop back to the start.

Perched on the ridge over Duluth, this park has perfect terrain for both mountain bikers and cross-country skiers, making it a very popular multiuse area. There are no facilities, and the only water you'll find is in small Merritt Creek, so bring water along.

SPIRIT MOUNTAIN

HIKING
BIKING
SKIING

Escape civilization to wander through a maple forest where you'll see no one all day.

Difficulty: Moderate

Length/Time: 1–6 miles; 1–12 hours

Hours/Fees: Open 24/7; free for hiking, $8 daily pass for nordic skiing

Getting There: *9535 West Skyline Pkwy.* Take Exit 249 off I-35 onto W. Skyline Pkwy. and head south for 0.4 mile to a T intersection. Turn left, staying on Skyline Pkwy. for 0.7 mile to the Nordic Center on the right. Enter and park on the road edge of the loop driveway. GPS: N46.7152°, W92.2222°

Contact: duluthxc.com/spirit-mtn-nordic-center

Additional Information: The trails begin in the grassy area north of the parking loop. The ski trails are wide, obvious, and easy to follow. At many intersections, you will find trail maps attached to trees with your current location indicated. You only need to decide which trail to explore. Trails may be covered in tall grass in summer, so long pants are a good idea, and hiking after a rain will mean wet shoes.

After hiking, you might want to visit Spirit Mountain Adventure Park, just west on Skyline Parkway, where you can try their alpine coaster, zipline, chairlift ride, or mini-golf.

Mountain bikers can barrel down the mountainside and ride the chairlift back up. When winter arrives, both alpine and nordic skiing take over the area.

Meander along the slow-moving waters of the St. Louis River before it empties into Lake Superior.

Difficulty: Easy, with no elevation gain and a clear, wide path

Length/Time: 4.3–6 miles; 1.5–3 hours

Hours/Fees: Open 24/7; free

Getting There: *7060 Grand Ave.* Take Exit 251B from I-35 onto Grand Ave. and head west for 1 mile. Immediately after you pass S. 72nd Ave. W. on your right, turn left into a paved trailhead parking area. GPS: N46.7248°, W92.1888°

Contact: 218-730-4300, duluthmn.gov/parks/parks-listing /western-waterfront-trail

Additional Information: Follow the trail across the railroad tracks to join the main trail heading southwest. At 1.75 miles, the trail veers left on a gravel road and passes a building before crossing Knowlton Creek on a footbridge. It then parallels railroad tracks at about 2.25 miles to the terminus of the trail at Spring Street. Turn right on Spring Street and follow it three blocks to a bridge crossing over the paved Munger Trail, a 70-mile bike route to the town of Hinckley. Take the Munger Trail northeast 1.25 miles to Pulaski Street. Turn right and walk through the parking area to the access trail, which connects to the main trail and back to your starting point.

Across Grand Avenue, the Lake Superior Zoo is a fun stop. Another interesting diversion is the Indian Point camp store, either at the very start or end of your hike. They advertise ice cream with a sign right by the trail.

At the corner of Fremont Street and Grand Avenue is the Lake Superior & Mississippi Railroad. You can take a 2-hour round-trip ride alongside the St. Louis River on the tracks you crossed earlier while hiking.

Best For . . .

BIRD-WATCHERS
- (8) Hawk Ridge Bird Observatory
- (9) Jay Cooke State Park
- (20) Western Waterfront

DOG WALKERS
- (7) Hartley Park
- (18) Piedmont
- (19) Spirit Mountain

FALL COLORS
- (2) Chester Park
- (5) Ely's Peak
- (8) Hawk Ridge Bird Observatory

HOT DAYS
- (3) Congdon Park
- (11) Lakewalk
- (16) Minnesota Point

KIDS
- (7) Hartley Park
- (11) Lakewalk
- (13) Lincoln Park

LAKE VIEWS
- (6) Enger Park
- (11) Lakewalk
- (16) Minnesota Point

SOLITUDE
- (14) Magney-Snively Natural Area
- (18) Piedmont
- (19) Spirit Mountain

TRAIL RUNNING
- (1) Brewer Park
- (7) Hartley Park
- (18) Piedmont

WATERFALLS
- (2) Chester Park
- (3) Congdon Park
- (12) Lester Park

WHEELCHAIR ACCESS
- (11) Lakewalk
- (15) Millennium Trail
- (17) Osaugie Trail